RL'4.7 No

W9-AFX-453

L:880

13.01 3/99

591
Eve

Crabapples

Really Weird Animals

DISCARDED

Tammy Everts & Bobbie Kalman

Crabtree Publishing Company

Crabapples

created by Bobbie Kalman

For Nancy

Editor-in-Chief
Bobbie Kalman

Writing team
Tammy Everts
Bobbie Kalman

Managing editor
Lynda Hale

Editors
Petrina Gentile
Niki Walker
Greg Nickles

Computer design
Lynda Hale

Color separations and film
Dot 'n Line Image Inc.

Printer
Worzalla Publishing Company

Illustrations
Jeannette McNaughton-Julich

Photographs
Nancy Adams/Tom Stack & Associates: front cover, pages 28-29
John Cancalosi/Tom Stack & Associates: pages 8-9, 16-17
Larry Foster/Earthviews: pages 10-11
Chip Isenhart/Tom Stack & Associates: page 25
G.C. Kelley/Tom Stack & Associates: page 4 (bottom)
M. Long/Visuals Unlimited: pages 18, 19
James McCullagh/Visuals Unlimited: page 15 (top)
Joe McDonald/Tom Stack & Associates: page 5 (bottom)
Gary Milburn/Tom Stack & Associates: pages 4 (top), 12, back cover
Brian Parker/Tom Stack & Associates: pages 14-15
G. Prance/Visuals Unlimited: page 6
Kevin Schafer/Tom Stack & Associates: page 7
Eric A. Soder/Tom Stack & Associates: pages 22-23
Milton H. Tierney, Jr./Visuals Unlimited: page 26
Roy Toft/Tom Stack & Associates: title page
Will Troyer/Visuals Unlimited: page 21
Barbara von Hoffman/Tom Stack & Associates: page 20
Dave Watts/Tom Stack & Associates: pages 5 (top), 24, 30

Crabtree Publishing Company

350 Fifth Avenue
Suite 3308
New York
N.Y. 10118

360 York Road, RR 4,
Niagara-on-the-Lake,
Ontario, Canada
L0S 1J0

73 Lime Walk
Headington
Oxford OX3 7AD
United Kingdom

Copyright © **1995 CRABTREE PUBLISHING COMPANY**. All rights reserved. No part of this publication may be reproduced, stored in a retrieval system or be transmitted in any form or by any means, electronic, mechanical, photocopying, recording, or otherwise, without the prior written permission of Crabtree Publishing Company.

Cataloging in Publication Data
Everts, Tammy, 1970-
   Really weird animals

(Crabapples)
Includes index.

ISBN 0-86505-627-7 (library bound) ISBN 0-86505-727-3 (pbk.)
The armadillo, narwhal, Tasmanian devil, and three-toed sloth are some of the unusual animals discussed in this book.

1. Animals - Juvenile literature. I. Kalman, Bobbie, 1947-   .
II. Title. III. Series: Kalman, Bobbie, 1947-   . Crabapples.

QL 49.E936 1995   j591   LC 95-39906
                                                    CIP

What is in this book?

So weird!

What is a really weird animal? In the animal world, no animal is actually weird. Every animal has an appearance or habits that make it different from other animals. To people, however, some animals seem more unusual than others.

Animals seem weird for many reasons. Some have unusual ways of finding or catching food. Others have strange ways of escaping from enemies, or **predators**. Still others have weird ways of getting from one place to another. An animal's "weirdness" often helps it survive in a harsh environment.

Three-toed sloth

It would take a three-toed sloth several minutes just to cross a road! Sloths cannot support themselves on their legs. Instead of walking, they drag themselves slowly along the ground.

Sloths are very comfortable in trees, where they spend most of their lives hanging upside down. Males often spend their whole life in the same tree!

Because a sloth cannot run away, it has other ways to protect itself from enemies. Its claws and legs grip branches so tightly that a predator cannot pull it down. A sloth's grip is so strong that it cannot be pulled from its branch— even when it is sleeping!

Armadillo

Armadillo is a Spanish word that means "little armored one." The armadillo's tough, hard skin makes this animal look as if it is wearing a suit of armor.

Some people believe that when an armadillo curls itself into a ball, its armor protects it from the claws and teeth of predators. This belief is not true. The armadillo's armor protects it from being scratched by thorns and branches, allowing it to escape into places where large predators cannot go.

An armadillo has unusual ways of crossing water. Sometimes it sinks to the bottom and walks across the riverbed. At other times, the armadillo swallows air until it is able to float. It then paddles across the river.

Narwhal

The narwhal's long horn makes this whale look very different from other whales. The "horn" is actually a tooth that grows out of an opening on a male narwhal's lip. The tooth can grow to be longer than a tall person! Some narwhals have two teeth. Sometimes female narwhals also grow a tooth.

Scientists do not know the purpose of the narwhal's tooth. Some say that it helps the narwhal catch food. Others believe that males use their tooth to fight for mates. Still others think that the tooth is just a decoration.

Hundreds of years ago, the narwhal's tooth was considered precious. People believed that it was the horn of a mythical animal called a unicorn.

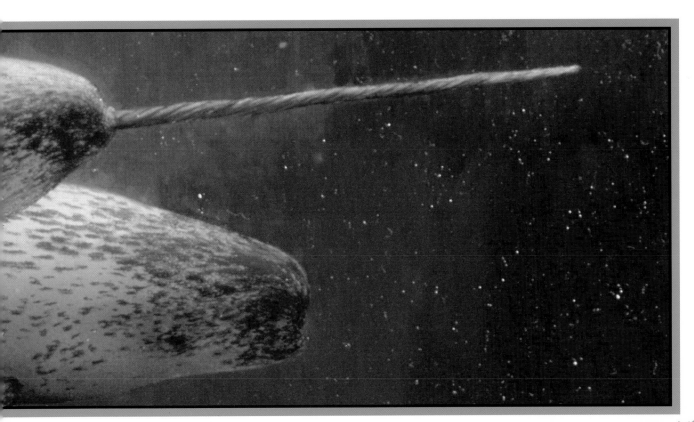

Tarsier

The tarsier lives high up in trees. Using its long, powerful legs, it travels by leaping from tree to tree. Its tail helps it steer in the air, and its long toes help it cling to branches.

The tarsier's large, round eyes allow it to see well at night. The eyes can only look straight ahead, but the tarsier can turn its head to see directly behind itself! This ability is useful for hunting, as well as for spotting predators. Tarsiers mainly eat insects, but they have been known also to hunt lizards, birds, and even poisonous snakes!

Although the tarsier shares its treetop home with snakes, it avoids being caught. Scientists believe the tarsier avoids snakes by lowering its body temperature while it rests. A snake locates its prey by sensing heat, so it is unable to find the cool tarsier.

Hagfish

The hagfish has no bones! Its muscular body has only a long piece of tough, bending tissue called **gristle**, which acts as its spine.

The hagfish is sometimes called a "slime eel" or "slime hag" because of the thick layer of slime, or mucus, that coats its skin. **Glands** down the sides of its body constantly produce mucus, making the hagfish so slippery that it can crawl inside its prey. When the single nostril of the hagfish becomes clogged with slime, it simply sneezes to clear its nose.

The hagfish has a poor sense of smell and is almost blind. Thin skin covers its eyes, which can sense only light and dark. Its mouth is surrounded by sensitive feelers called **barbels**. The barbels are its only means of searching for prey.

When a hagfish finds a dead or sick fish, it uses its toothless mouth and raspy tongue to burrow into the fish. Once inside, it sucks out the flesh.

Tuatara

The tuatara is the oldest species of **reptile**. Scientists have found fossils of its ancestors from millions of years ago. Tuataras are called "living fossils." They have changed, or **adapted**, very little over the years because conditions on their island home have not changed.

Other toothed animals have separate teeth that grow out of their jawbones. A tuatara's teeth and jawbone are all one piece. The teeth are actually jagged edges of bone that poke through the gums.

The tuatara has a third eye on top of its head! You cannot see this eye because it is under a layer of clear skin called a **membrane**. The eye cannot see objects, but it can sense movement and light.

Aardwolf

The aardwolf is the smallest member of the hyena family. It looks like a wolf, but it does not behave as wolves do. Wolves hunt rabbits, deer, and moose. The aardwolf prefers to eat antlike insects called termites.

Termites are active at night. They scurry along the hard-packed earth of the **savannah**, looking for food. Aardwolves are also busy at night as they hunt for termites. An aardwolf has excellent hearing—it can find termites by listening for their tiny "footsteps."

When an aardwolf finds some termites, it catches them on its sticky, snakelike tongue. It can eat as many as 200,000 termites at one meal!

Warthog

Some people consider the warthog one of the stranger looking animals in the world. This may be because of the wartlike bumps on the hog's face or the curved tusks that grow from its nose.

A warthog has a short neck and long front legs. It cannot eat standing up. When the warthog eats roots and short grass, it has to kneel on its front knees and shuffle along the ground. Pads of tough skin protect its knees.

Capybara

The capybara is the world's largest **rodent**. It can weigh as much as a grown person! The capybara's name means "master of the grasses."

The capybara is also called a "water hog." It does not actually look like a pig, but it does enjoy being in the water. It spends hot afternoons sitting in the water with only its eyes, ears, and nose poking above the surface. Its muscular legs and strong webbed feet are perfectly designed for swimming.

When the capybara is hungry, it does not have to go far for a snack. It dines on the plants and grasses that grow along the edge of the water.

Tasmanian devil

The Tasmanian devil is named for its loud screech, which is terrifying even from a distance. It lives on the island of Tasmania, off the coast of Australia. Like many Australian animals, the Tasmanian devil is a **marsupial**. Female marsupials have a pouch on their body where their babies eat and sleep.

FRIENDSHIP JR. HIGH
LEARNING CENTER
550 ELIZABETH LANE
DES PLAINES, IL 60018

24

The Tasmanian devil looks like a small, chunky bear. Despite its fierce-sounding name, this animal is not a vicious killer. Its powerful jaws and sharp teeth allow it to eat almost anything it finds—from socks and shoes to tin cans and car parts! It prefers to eat **carrion**, or animals that are already dead, but sometimes it hunts and eats other Tasmanian devils!

Zorilla

The zorilla looks like its cousin the skunk, and it smells even worse. In fact, the zorilla is considered the smelliest animal in the world! It sprays a bad-smelling liquid from **scent glands** near its tail. A zorilla marks its territory with its scent. The scent also keeps other animals from stealing the zorilla's meal of eggs, insects, and small animals.

zorilla

The zorilla's smell is its only means of defense. It can spray a predator as far as five meters (16 feet) away. The spray blinds an attacker long enough for the zorilla to escape. To avoid being sprayed, lions and other large predators run away from the small zorilla.

skunk

Proboscis monkey

The proboscis monkey is easy to
recognize. Even if you did not notice
its large nose, you would not miss
the loud honking sound it makes!

The male proboscis monkey has a larger nose than the female. Males honk to frighten away predators and to warn other proboscis monkeys of danger. When the monkey honks, its nose shoots upward.

Proboscis monkeys live in large groups. They spend most of their time in trees that are near water. If they are in danger from enemies, they often jump into the water and swim away to safety. At night, proboscis monkeys sleep side by side in a row along a branch.

Wombat

The wombat is one of the largest burrowing animals. It makes its home under the ground. The wombat is a marsupial. Unlike most marsupials, which have pouches that open toward the mother's face, a wombat's pouch opens near her tail. When the wombat digs, dirt cannot get into her pouch.

Words to know

adapt To become different to suit a new environment

barbel A feeler on the face of some types of fish

carrion Dead and decaying meat

gland A sac inside the body that produces a liquid

gristle A tough, flexible tissue

marsupial A family of animals, the female of which carries her babies in a pouch on her body

membrane A thin, transparent layer of skin

predator An animal that hunts and kills other animals for food

reptile A family of animals that includes snakes, lizards, alligators, and turtles

rodent A family of small, gnawing mammals that includes mice, squirrels, and rats

savannah Grassland that contains few trees

scent gland A sac inside an animal's body that contains a bad-smelling liquid

Index

What is in the picture?

Here is more information about the photographs in this book.

3 4 5 6 7 8 9 0 Printed in the U.S.A. 4 3 2 1 0 9 8